CONTENTS

4	The autism gallery
6	*Real Life Story* Naughty but nice
7	*Real Life Story* A tale of two brothers
8	Quiz: what sort of brother or sister are you?
10	Why does he do that?
12	Fall-out flashpoints
13	How do you feel?
14	Top 10 tips for getting on
15	What can we do together?
16	Friends
18	Mind your Ps and Qs – communicating with your sibling
20	Avoiding rows and coping with meltdown
22	*Real Life Story* Living with my brother
23	A great night out
24	Stressed out or chilled out – how do you cope with stress?
26	Coping with parents
27	*Real Life Story* Being protective... + Puzzle it out
28	Questions people often ask
30	*Real Life Story* What's the matter with your brother?
31	Puzzle it out + A great night out (part two)
32	Bullying
34	Problem page
36	You can't always blame autism – 10 irritating things about siblings
37	Where to find help + A great night out (part three)
38	*Real Life Story* Living with my sister
39	Terms you may come across

You've probably heard the words autism, Asperger syndrome and autism spectrum disorder (ASD) as your brother or sister may already have been given a diagnosis of one of these, or may be getting one soon. Autism and Asperger syndrome are parts of the autism spectrum, and they are all terms used to describe the difficulties faced by people with the condition.

Difficulties with:

- communication – talking, understanding and using facial expressions, tone of voice, gestures, body language, jokes, sarcasm and following instructions

- socialising – understanding what other people think, feel, believe or know, as well as mixing with other people and making friends

- thinking in a flexible way – adapting to new situations or change, especially when they are sudden or unexpected – routines and obsessions are very important

- processing information – more time is needed to understand and react or respond during conversations

- sensory experiences – may be particularly sensitive to some sights, sounds, smells, textures, tastes and temperatures, finding them hard to bear or, on the other hand, may find them particularly fascinating.

All of these difficulties affect their lives and how they are when they're with other people.

The autism spectrum is wide-ranging: some people are affected more by their condition than others. It spans from people with severe learning difficulties to some very able people: rich to poor, fat to thin, quiet to loud. The things people with autism find hard are things that we may all find hard at times and this can help us to understand what they experience to some extent. But the important thing to remember is that everyone is an individual.

Take a quick look at the thumbnail portraits opposite of young people on the autism spectrum. See if you can spot any similarities with your brother or sister.

Name	Age	Diagnosis	Description
Jonathan	10	Asperger syndrome	Loves Dr Who and knows everything about it – actors, plots, dates. Quiet. Attends local primary school, keeps himself to himself. Good at singing but doesn't really connect with the other children, unless they ask him about Dr Who.
Craig	13	Autism spectrum disorder (ASD) with attention deficit hyperactivity disorder (ADHD)	Dynamite. Never stops talking, moving. Loses temper easily, but can be very affectionate. Has been excluded from school twice. Wants friends but often loses them because he insists they do things his way and he gets upset when they break his rules.
Khalida	14	Autism spectrum	Good at telling stories – mum doesn't know when to believe what she tells her about school. Likes dancing, acting and role play. Tries to be like her older sister and gets frustrated because she wants more friends and finds it hard to make and keep them. Other young people find her slightly puzzling and sometimes irritating.
Jack	12	Autism spectrum disorder	Jack appears to daydream a lot at school. He smiles and laughs to himself a lot which makes others wary of him. Collects DVDs of comedy shows like 'Have I Got News For You', watches them over and over and enjoys telling others about them. Struggles to focus on things which other people find important, eg football, rock bands.
Chrissy	12	Autism	Chrissy attends a special school where she loves the routine. Main interest is food – especially McDonald's. Gets very impatient if kept waiting for meals and frustrated and angry if routine is changed suddenly. Only knows some words and rarely speaks, but can repeat bits from her favourite books and videos. Loves playing chase with her dad and older brother but otherwise doesn't mix much with them – prefers her own world.
Kenny	11	No diagnosis yet but dyspraxia or autism spectrum disorder mentioned as a possibility	Struggles at school because he finds writing difficult, though he can read quite well. Finds school very tiring and often gets frustrated with other children and with teachers when they expect more of him than he can give. At home recovers by watching DVDs, playing computer games. Never talks about school at home.
Hussein	14	Autism	A tall guy with a lovely smile, but unable to talk very much. Laughs a lot to himself and likes to collect pictures of cars which he enjoys showing to people. Sometimes gets very distressed, especially in noisy places, and bites his knuckle so that it has a patch of tough red skin on it.

You may recognise some of the situations in the real life stories on these two pages and on pages 22, 27, 30 and 28.

Naughty but nice

One sister writes…

For the past 11 years, I have been following my brother around train stations, the Natural History Museum and the Science Museum.

For the past 11 years, I've had to put up with Noddy, Postman Pat, Thomas the Tank Engine, Pingu and Bob the Builder.

When he's in a bad mood, it's not just a strop. There's screaming, shouting, repeating, "I'm not in a bad mood, no darling!" But when Lawrence is in a good mood, he makes me laugh, a lot. Sometimes I'm crying because I've been laughing so much.

You would generally think that every girl loves shopping, but I hate it, unless I'm with my friends. One time I can remember clearly we were on the escalator in a clothes shop. I was talking to Lawrence and he punched me. Now, his attitude has completely changed, so he doesn't punch me. Instead, we cannot walk out of a shop empty-handed.

Lawrence went away for three days on a Year 6 trip – I thought I wouldn't miss him. But I did. Mum and I just sat there in silence at dinner. What if he wanted to go home as soon as he got there? I really did miss him. When Lawrence got back, he didn't say hello to me. He just went straight to the computer.

Living with Lawrence makes me look at life differently.

A tale of two brothers

Damion has Asperger syndrome and his brother Dean is three years younger than him. I've known them both for over seven years. I spoke to them separately, but asked them the same questions about their life growing up together, now that they are both in their twenties and living independently.

What are your main memories of growing up – good and bad?

Damion: I felt different from others at school. I didn't understand whether they were laughing at me or with me. I was bullied a bit but not often and only verbally. I got on better when I changed schools and went to one where classes were smaller and more help was given. I had a few friends at school but they didn't come back to my house.

Dean: At mainstream school he was a real little hell-raiser, getting into fights because he was bullied and picked on. I realised he didn't know any better – if others swore at him, he just swore back – so if I saw him I just tried to drag him out. Once he changed schools he didn't need to get angry any more. He learnt kickboxing and it was a channel for his anger. After three months, I started learning with him and six years later we still go together.

How did you get on with your brother?

Damion: I got on with my brother OK. We used to play on the PlayStation together and watch TV. We liked building bonfires in the summer and when I started kickboxing he eventually came along with me – and still does. I don't remember arguing with him – except for play fighting. I do remember him and mum arguing though! We get on well together now though neither of us lives at home any more. I go round to the pub where he works a couple of times a week and have a drink at the bar with him.

Dean: Damion took up a lot of my time. When we were younger, he had to come out with me and I would help him with crossing the road. My mum needed a break. I wasn't always happy about having him with me though because he used to flap his hands. He had some embarrassing obsessions. One was car washes – he'd stand on the main street flapping his hands as he watched the cars go through.

How do you think Asperger syndrome has affected your life?

Damion: Things have got better as I've got older. I feel I've grown out of it. I don't care if people are laughing any more and I can cotton on to what people are saying to me. I do still sometimes find it difficult reading things – I tend to take the literal meaning and not get the hidden meaning. I tried to do an IQ test and couldn't work out how to solve one of the problems in it.

Dean: I never thought I'd stop looking after him but now he has control of his feelings and actions and he has some good friends without me. I did get frustrated when I was younger, but I tried to work at things with him and make it positive and not negative.

What about now?

Damion: I'm now a dad – though I don't live with my girlfriend any more. I'm getting used to it and like to play games with my son when I see him: 'peek-a-boo' and stuff like that. I make him jump and laugh. I don't feel the need to explain Asperger syndrome to anyone – I wouldn't know how to. I'm happy with who I am.

Dean: Now he can choose between right and wrong and chooses not to be with anyone who doesn't respect him. People take him for who he is. ■

QUIZ: What sort of BROTHER or SISTER are YOU?

Have a look at the situations below and choose the reaction nearest to the one you think you would have. Reactions vary according to mood or tiredness so you may find all four descriptions fit you at some time. So just pick the best fit and try to be honest!

1. **Your brother is screaming in the next room and your mum is down the garden. Do you:**

…yell at him to stop because you can't hear the DVD you're watching?	…stop what you're doing and go to see what the matter is?	…shout out of the window for your mum to come – and carry on watching the DVD?	…pretend you haven't heard?

2. **You come back into the house after an evening out and find your brother in your room looking at your stuff. Do you:**

…put on a silly voice and pretend to be a policeman arresting him for trespassing?	…check that all your things are still there and tell him to get out?	…yell, "Get out you ****!!", grab him, shove him out of the room and slam the door?	…sit down and look at the stuff with him, then find a DVD he can go and watch somewhere else?

3. **Your sister is very anxious and not sleeping well so has just got up noisily to go to the loo for the third time in the night and woken you up. You look at your watch and see that it's 3am. Do you:**

…find your ear plugs, put a pillow over your head and try to get back to sleep, cursing inwardly?	…get up and shout at her to shut up – you've only just got off to sleep!?	…go and offer her your lava lamp that helped soothe you before exams?	…turn up your iPod which you left on when you fell asleep and hope that your favourite music drowns out the noise?

4. **Your dad is shouting at your brother for not getting ready for school quickly enough. You know your brother hates being hurried. Do you:**

…tell your dad to chill out or there'll be a major tantrum?	…feel relieved that you're not the one in trouble for a change and hope that you miss the school bus?	…join in with your dad, threatening to confiscate your brother's favourite DVD to make him hurry?	…slip out of the back door quickly before you get shouted at, too?

5. **You are going 10-pin bowling with some friends and your parents have asked you to take your brother along with you. Do you:**

…plead with your mum not to make you take him because you know he'll only embarrass you?	…agree, then phone up a friend who is good with your brother so that she can help look after him with you?	…say that's ok even though you feel taken advantage of – then feel guilty for being so mean?	…say "No way!" and storm out of the room?

8

6. **You are watching a football match on TV with your dad and are totally engrossed but your sister keeps tapping irritatingly on the back of the chair. Do you:**

...shout, "Shut up will you, you ****!"?	...ask your sister if she would like to play with a piece of Blu-Tak to keep her hands occupied?	...go off and watch it on the TV upstairs?	...start humming the theme music of your sister's favourite DVD in the hope that she'll go and watch it upstairs?

7. **It's Sunday lunchtime and it's roast dinner - your favourite. Your sister is very fussy about hygiene and won't eat her dinner because she says you didn't wash your hands and have touched her plate. Do you:**

...explain to her that there are germs all over the place which don't do any harm – they may even help her to build up her immunity, so chill?	...lose your temper with her and shout that you can have dirty hands if you want – it's your home too; why can't she be normal!?	...pretend to eat one of her potatoes, then act being violently sick and laugh when she screams because you think she's putting it all on?	...appeal to your parents to tell her to shut up and mind her own business – they're your hands?

8. **It's your mum's birthday and your dad has organised a surprise party for her. Your brother lets the secret out by asking her if there'll be time to go swimming as usual before the party. Do you:**

...decide that you will never, ever, get a birthday card or present for him on his birthday – that'll teach him?	...shrug and think to yourself that you're not surprised – it wasn't a very sensible idea of dad's anyway – mum would've hated the surprise?	...grit your teeth and silently wish you had a different brother or sister who could help you organise a surprise party without ruining it?	...butt in quickly and start talking about an 18th party you are going to and hope that mum thinks he's talking about that?

HOW TO INTERPRET YOUR RESULTS

Count up how many answers of each colour you have and see if you recognise yourself in the descriptions below.

MAINLY BLUE	MAINLY RED	MAINLY GREEN	MAINLY PURPLE
You're very responsible for your age and try to help your brother/sister whenever you can. To make sure you give as much attention to your own needs, it's important to let your parents know what you want to do and to set aside time for your own interests and relaxation, whether it's a dance class, a football match, shopping or a trip to the cinema, or just hanging out with your friends.	You're laid back and fun, with a busy social life. You care about your brother or sister but usually prefer being with your friends. To make spending time with your brother/sister more fun, it's a good idea to find something that you both enjoy doing. It could be going for a meal, listening to music, walking or a martial arts class – whatever you like.	You're fairly quiet and get on with your own interests. You tend to leave your brother/sister to your parents because it's easier and you like having your own space. To find a less stressful way of spending time with your brother/sister, you could try watching a film that you both like, or playing a computer game or a board game. Make sure you get some time to yourself too.	You get really fed up with the way your brother/sister interferes with your life – and that's pretty natural. What could really help is trying a different way of talking to him/her, to explain what you're doing and why, and how much time you need. If you need some time to yourself, you could promise to spend time doing his/her favourite thing together afterwards.

Why does he do that??

Explaining your brother's behaviour to your friends

Have you ever felt the need to explain your brother's behaviour to your friends – for instance when he's done something really embarrassing in front of them or had a tantrum for no obvious reason? Your friends may think he's weird or believe he's being deliberately selfish, destructive or awkward when these things happen. After all, he looks the same as everyone else. What they need to understand is that the brains of people on the autism spectrum work in a different way – and this affects their behaviour and reactions.

There's no single right or easy way to explain autism spectrum disorder because everyone on the autism spectrum is an individual with individual characteristics. However, it might be an idea to mention a few key facts – just as we mentioned on page 4 – that fit everyone on the spectrum.

If friends ask and are really interested it can be helpful to give them a leaflet or card with a brief explanation of autism

'Asperger syndrome (AS) is a condition that affects the brain. People who have the condition have difficulty interacting with other people, developing friendships and communication effectively. They also have difficulty with understanding body language and non-verbal communication. There can be difficulties when there is significant change to their routine or faced with a situation they are unfamiliar with. On the plus side, people with AS tend to have good memories, extensive knowledge about subjects they are interested in and are generally very reliable.'

or Asperger syndrome written down – The National Autistic Society produces both, see the publications section of the NAS website www.autism.org.uk/shop. In some cases, more able young people on the autism spectrum may be able to write their own personalised explanation. The one above is written by Anthony, who has Asperger syndrome.

It might be a good idea for you to create your own explanation if your brother or sister can't write one him/herself. Apart from anything else it will help you to be clearer in your own mind next time someone asks ■

Here's a rough guide as an example. You could start by ticking the things in italics that apply to your brother/sister and adding personal examples.

MY BROTHER/SISTER HAS
Autism spectrum disorder
Autism
Asperger syndrome
It is not an illness, or something he/she can grow out of, though things can keep on improving for him/her well into adult life.

THIS MEANS S/HE HAS COMMUNICATION DIFFICULTIES, EG
Having conversations
Knowing how close to stand to people
Using the right words
Understanding what people say
Expressing his/her feelings
Listening to others for a long time

S/HE ALSO HAS DIFFICULTIES SOCIALISING, EG
Understanding the way others feel
Knowing the social 'rules', eg the right amount of eye contact
Being part of a group
Meeting new people
Knowing why others laugh at him/her
Knowing when others are bored

S/HE NEEDS ORDER AND A FAMILIAR ROUTINE
Likes doing things in a particular order
Has difficulty learning a new method of doing something
Has interests or even obsessions which take up a lot of time every day
Reads/watches/plays the same things over and over

WHAT HELPS HIM/HER
Not asking too many questions
Allowing time for him/her to take things in
Making expectations clear – writing them down if necessary
Being prepared in advance for a change of plan
Being told why you got upset

WHAT S/HE IS GOOD AT
Remembering numbers
Being truthful and honest
Mimicking
Concentrating for hours on one thing (own interest)
Never being malicious
Being determined
Taking people at face value

Fall-out Flashpoints

Living with a brother or sister on the autism spectrum is a lot like living with any brother or sister, in that it's sometimes tough. But the flashpoints causing rows can be different. See if any of these real-life examples sound familiar.

You are due to go out to a party in five minutes but your dad says he can't take you because your sister is having a tantrum and can't be left.

Your brother loves paper – especially shiny paper – and has just scrunched up some of your best art project paper to fiddle with.

Your brother keeps bringing you his favourite magazine for you to read to him even though you are exhausted and just wanting to chill out.

Your brother trashes your DVDs because he thinks you've got the one your parents have hidden to stop him damaging it by re-playing the same clip over and over.

You've come in from school shattered and there's nothing to eat. Mum has locked the fridge and larder to stop your sister getting at the food she's prepared for guests at the weekend and the key has gone missing or been hidden.

You are about to walk your brother round to his swimming lesson on your way to a friend's and he has a tantrum because you shouted at him for making you late.

You can't finish your coursework because your sister got frustrated with the computer and broke it by hurling the keyboard across the room.

You have some friends round for the evening and your brother keeps coming into the room and asking them the same question over and over and won't get the message that you don't want him there.

Your brother saw you smoking in the back garden and immediately told your mum because he knows it's bad for you and thinks you're going to die.

Your sister has 'tidied up' your make up and lined it up along the window sill because it wasn't put away and has lost your best lipstick.

Top tips for getting on

This can apply to either your brother or your sister

1. Never rush them if they're in the middle of doing something – it's pointless!

2. Accept that they need to do the same things over and over to relax – it's not boring to them!

3. Go back to explain why you got cross after a row – when you have calmed down a bit.

4. Warn them if you know you are going to do something different from normal – it will save a lot of grief.

5. Remember to give plenty of time for a response if you ask something – as long as ten seconds.

6. Get a lock for your bedroom door if you don't want your stuff touched.

7. Don't ask for an honest opinion – eg 'Does my bum looks big in these jeans?' – unless you want the truth!

8. Try communicating using pictures or writing – email is good. It gives more time for them to understand what you are saying and to reply.

9. Include them when you're talking to the rest of the family – even if you're not sure they understand what you're saying.

10. Try to set aside some time regularly to do something with them that they enjoy.

☐ Do you agree with these tips?
☐ Are there any tips you'd add?

Email your suggestion to **publications@nas.org.uk** with the subject 'Top sibling tip'.

> "When my brother was 14 there was an obsession for John Denver's music… I started to teach him the guitar, a task that seemed impossible due to his lack of coordination and academic ability, but in time he began to excel …we discovered he could imitate any chord or sound he heard. Today Matthew communicates best through his music."
> **Alison**
> (from the NAS website)

> "Generally I got on quite well with my sister. We did a lot of activities together such as horse riding, badminton etc. I think she understood the difficulties I had in certain areas and was usually sympathetic. I was aware of some of the things that were happening in her life. I did get annoyed when I found that there were things she could do that I couldn't, or if she knew something I didn't. There were also arguments when we both wanted to watch TV (different programmes) at the same time."
> **Anthony**
> (who has Asperger syndrome)

 # ...What can we DO TOGETHER?

It's ok **not** to spend lots of time doing stuff with your brother or sister – plenty of people don't – but if you find something you really enjoy and can do it with them regularly, even for just a few minutes, **it can help you get along better.**

SWIMMING
Good for you anyway – and has the advantage of not being team-based or competitive.

MARTIAL ARTS
Useful for discouraging bullies as well as for general fitness, whether you choose kick boxing, tae kwondo, ju jitsu or any other.........

HORSE RIDING
If you like the fresh air or love animals and have a good riding school nearby, this could be a fun thing to do together.

WATCHING DVDs
Although your tastes may differ there should be some overlap – comedies for instance – which can then be shared topics of conversation.

EATING OUT
This can be a way of broadening your brother's or sister's horizons – especially if they don't go out much socially, even Macdonalds!

LOOKING AT FAMILY PHOTOS
Either in albums or on screen – it doesn't matter – will make the most of your shared memories and could give you a laugh too!

TELLING JOKES
Especially puns or KNOCK KNOCK jokes – WHICH YOUR BROTHER OR SISTER MAY BE BETTER AT REMEMBERING AND TELLING THAN YOU!

MAKING MUSIC
Singing or playing an instrument together can be fun, but is also a way of communicating, even with a brother or sister who cannot speak!

COMPUTER GAMES
...can teach all kinds of skills – but stick to ones where you're fairly evenly matched or you'll end up **fighting!**

BOARD GAMES & CARD GAMES
There are lots of games that give people with autism a chance to excel, ranging from **chess** to **snap!**

WALKING
...Provides a non-demanding opportunity to chat and can be a way of sharing hobbies like birdwatching, geology or others.

FRIENDS

The people you hang around with can make the difference between happiness and misery.
If your best friend suddenly stops speaking to you or your boyfriend dumps you, it can feel like the end of the world.

Any relationship can affect the way you feel. A cheery 'hello' from a bus driver on a dull morning can make you feel marginally better about travelling to school or college. A friend offering to share a taxi on a night out can make it easier going to a new bar. A casual acquaintance saying 'I like your hair' can make you feel great.

But are you aware of all the people in your life and how they affect your happiness?

Look at the 'Levels of friendship' table opposite and think about your own relationships. Obviously these can change as people get closer or more distant, but just think about today.

● Who would you put in your column for each category?

● How many friends are very close?

You won't necessarily have anyone intimate. It could be that one of your parents is still that person. Or maybe not. You may have loads of quite close friends

> "School was difficult socially and I would seek sanctuary in the music room at lunch times, as people connected with music seemed to be more on my wavelength. As a teenager, I threw myself into my schoolwork, rarely going out socially or doing much other than study, music practice and various orchestra rehearsals."
> **Lisa**
> (a young woman with Asperger syndrome)

but no one very close. Girls often have more close relationships than boys and some people are perfectly happy with one or two friends. There are no rules. We are all different.

It only matters if you want more friends than you have and don't know how to go about moving people up from being distant to close, eg from being someone you see on the bus each day, to someone you go out with and whose house you go to several times a week.

People on the autism spectrum generally have more difficulty making friends than other people because of their difficulties communicating. ■

Whether we have autism or not we still need to spend time making and building friendships. If we go to places where we meet like-minded people they may eventually change from acquaintances into true friends. People with autism have greater difficulty doing this without help.

LEVELS OF FRIENDSHIP

Fill in the table below for yourself, and then do the same for your brother/sister who has autism. Think about the difference between you.

Even though good friends are so important to our personal happiness, we don't get friendship training. We're not all equally skilled when it comes to making and keeping friends. It's possible to be really brainy, eg good at maths or music, but not good at making friends. People on the autism spectrum have particular difficulty understanding people and therefore understanding friends.

Relationship	Description	Eg	You	Your sibling
1. Intimate	Someone you share everything with – joys, sorrows, secrets, hopes, fears. The first person you want to share good news with. Someone you trust completely. Someone who knows you completely & who accepts you for who you are.	Boyfriend. Girlfriend. Parent.		
2. Close	Someone you spend a lot of time with and whose company you enjoy. Someone who notices if you aren't around and phones to see if you're ok if you don't turn up at school. You go to each other's houses quite a lot and miss each other if you're not around. It could also be a sister or brother.	Best friend. Family member.		
3. Quite close	Someone who is part of your circle, wider family or gang. One of the crowd you hang around with. Someone you like to be with but you don't go round to their home, eg someone you work with or sit with at school or college. You have common interests which you talk about quite a bit.	Mate, one of your crowd. Cousin.		
4. Acquaintance	Someone you see fairly regularly but wouldn't go out of your way to meet. Someone you travel to school, college or work with. You pass the time of day with them but don't discuss personal things.	In your tutor group at school or college. At sports club.		
5. Distant friend	Someone who is important to you but far away. Maybe they have moved house or you met them online. You share a lot by email, in chat rooms or on Facebook. You have common interests but rarely meet.	Friend who moved house. Online friend.		
6. Professionals	People paid to help you. You may see them frequently or only very occasionally depending on their job. They may feel close because they know you very well and you like them. But you know less about them.	Doctor. Teacher. Youth group leader.		

DON'T...

...SAY: "...BUT I ALWAYS DO THIS AND YOU ALWAYS DO THAT" WHEN YOUR BROTHER/SISTER ANNOYS YOU — UNLESS IT'S TRUE. THEY'RE LIKELY TO LOSE THEIR TEMPER IF IT'S NOT.

...SAY THINGS LIKE: "DID YOU GET OUT OF THE WRONG SIDE OF THE BED THIS MORNING?" AND EXPECT A CIVIL ANSWER!

...SAY: "I WISH SHE WAS DEAD!" WHEN YOU'RE CROSS WITH SOMEONE. YOUR BROTHER/SISTER MAY THINK YOU ARE PLANNING MURDER!

...BE SARCASTIC. SAYING: "THAT WAS A GREAT HELP" WHEN THEY'VE, SAY, SPILT A DRINK, CAN CONFUSE THEM.

...ASK RHETORICAL QUESTIONS (ONES THAT DON'T NEED ANSWERS), LIKE: "WHY ARE YOU SO STUPID?" WHEN YOU DON'T REALLY WANT THEM TO REPLY.

...GENERALIZE! SAYING: "EVERYONE KNOWS THAT!" MIGHT MAKE THEM BELIEVE THEY'RE THE ONLY PERSON IN THE WHOLE WORLD WHO DOESN'T UNDERSTAND.

Another problem I have is when people don't say what they really mean.

Sometimes I get confused and switch off which must appear really rude, but I don't really understand small talk and therefore never know what to say...

as it seems pointless.

Lisa

AVOIDING ROWS AND CO[...]

The best way to cope with anger and aggression is to see it coming and avoid it. That's not always possible...

LONG BEFORE...

JUST BEFORE...

Think of ways to communicate...
Do things together.
Use simple language.
Give time for a response.
Notice what causes stress.

Notice signs of tension...
Try to divert to something "safer".
Use simple language.

Say as little as possible...
Don't shout.
Stay calm.
Tell your parents.

Move away.
Put your safety first.
Look after people.
Remove anything that [could] cause damage or h[...]
Get an adult.

20

...PING WITH MELT DOWN

JUST AFTER... LONG AFTER...

IT BE THROWN OR USED TO ANYONE.

LET YOUR PARENTS DEAL WITH IT... THINK WHAT CAN CALM THE SITUATION (MUSIC, DVDs ETC). DON'T SAY ANYTHING, — NOW IS NOT THE TIME! DON'T BLAME ANYONE.

TALK TO YOUR PARENTS ABOUT WHAT HAPPENED... BUT NOT IN FRONT OF YOUR BROTHER OR SISTER. TRY TO REMEMBER WHAT TRIGGERED THE INCIDENT.

DISCUSS WHAT HAPPENED... WITH SOMEONE YOU TRUST - WHO UNDERSTANDS AUTISM (E.G. A SIBLING SUPPORT GROUP). BE HONEST. DON'T FEEL GUILTY!

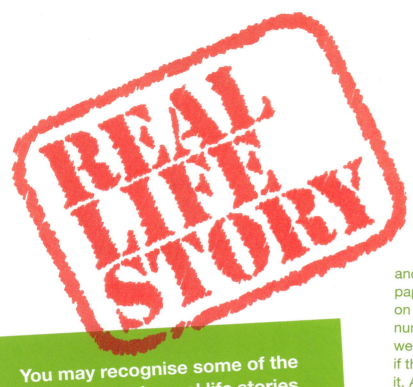

You may recognise some of the situations in the real life stories included here and on pages 6, 7, 27, 30 and 38.

Living with my brother

Fiona taught for many years in special schools and was a deputy head. She is a trained counsellor and now works as an autism consultant. She remembers the amusing side of growing up with a brother who has autism...

Adrian, my brother, is two years older than me and has autism with a severe learning difficulty. I always accepted that Adrian was 'different' because my parents explained to me very early on that he had this thing called 'autism' and that it made his brain 'poorly' and this was why he did 'funny things' and behaved in odd ways.

Adrian had difficulty communicating with others but had a fantastic rote memory. He was fascinated by numbers from an early age and would rote count over and over again, chanting the numbers he had learnt and writing them repetitively on pieces of paper or on the walls of our bungalow or on the furniture! He insisted on tracing the numbers on people's gate posts when we went out and would become extremely upset if there was a gate post with no number on it. Another thing he liked doing was repeating the same word, phrase or action, sometimes even in potentially dangerous circumstances such as in the middle of the road.

He went through phases of 'sensory-based' behaviours when he would become very preoccupied with putting things in his mouth and tapping them against his teeth, licking objects (including walls and floors) and smelling seats where people had been sitting!

Another obsessive interest etched in my memory is the 'floating vegetation and mop' ritual which lasted for quite some considerable time. For some inexplicable reason, Adrian became fixated on any vegetable matter in the house. While eating an apple for example, I would be acutely aware that Adrian would be watching and waiting for the moment when I would reach to throw the core into the waste bin. Quick as a flash, he would retrieve the core, race into the kitchen, fill the sink with water and float the core in it. Soon, all kinds of vegetable matter was destined to join the floating core – lettuce leaves, banana skins, orange peel, the works.

Mum and Dad valiantly tried to intervene in this annoying ritual but this only served to make Adrian more determined in his quest. As a final flourish, the ritual became complete when Adrian started to insist that the mop had to stand up at all times in the sink full of assorted vegetation and water. This ritual became so firmly entrenched that as a family, we finally admitted defeat and lived permanently with a floating mass of vegetation in our kitchen sink, resplendent with mop which we moved aside when we needed to do the washing up and dutifully replaced when we had finished, all under the watchful eye of Adrian himself, of course!

I look back at my early years growing up with him with great fondness. He may have driven me to distraction at times, embarrassed me in front of my friends, caused me anguish and frustration at other times, but I wouldn't have changed him for the world. He is my brother – unique, quirky and truly inspirational! ■

2. THEN I...

- Scream/shout
- Cry/sob/wail!
- Swear/curse
- Stamp/kick/hit/lash out
- Throw/smash something
- Slam doors/bang fist
- Storm off/run away
- Bite tongue/fist/nails
- Flap/pace up & down
- Carry on with what I was doing

3. LATER I...

- Phone Mum/friend
- Laugh and pretend I'm OK
- Blame someone/something else
- Go shopping/go out
- Eat/drink too much
- Stop eating
- Smoke
- Do something rash & make it worse
- Sulk/hide/stay in bed/go online
- Stay in a foul mood
- Relapse and act like a child
- Tell myself I'm useless
- Worry/have sleep problems
- Can't concentrate

4. I COULD...

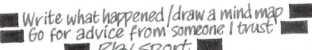

- Write what happened/draw a mind map
- Go for advice from someone I trust
- Play sport
- Do something creative (music/drama)
- Book a treat/night out
- Go and help someone worse off
- Have a good laugh with a friend
- Stroke the dog/cat
- Find someone else in the same position & talk
- Go for a long walk with someone
- Learn relaxation techniques

DONE THAT? ✓

- NOW LOOK AT THE LISTS AGAIN.
- THINK ABOUT YOUR BROTHER/SISTER, THE LAST TIME THEY WERE ANGRY, AGITATED OR AFRAID. PUT A **CROSS** BESIDE ALL THE THINGS THAT APPLY TO **THEM**...
- HOW DIFFERENT ARE THEY TO **YOU**?

TRY THIS:
Next time you are stressed, try some of the things in the "I COULD..." list - they may help you (and your brother) to cope (and chill!)

Parents

Parents can be very annoying, very irritating and very demanding as well as being a rock when we need them. You may get on brilliantly with yours all the time, in which case you are in the lucky minority, or you may feel they have failed you in a big way. Most people have problems with parents at some time or other and most parents have problems with their children sometimes too. But how do you cope when things are going badly between you? Here are some ideas to help smooth the troubled waters.

You may recognise some of the situations in the real life stories included here and on pages 6, 7, 22, 30 and 38.

Being protective

Carys, aged 16, writes about her brother

My brother Thomas is 19 and has autism as well as Tourette's*, OCD* and ADHD*. He is one of the most loving people I know and I shall miss him dearly when he goes to residential college this year.

Probably the most annoying thing for me about Thomas is my Mum's protection over him - he can't be out of eyesight! And this is how she treats me sometimes. It's hard going out with friends because she wants a constant commentary on where I am, what I'm doing and who I'm with! My Dad is less intrusive into my everyday life but he's more laid back about Tom, too, and my parents sometimes argue about what Tom can and can't do.

I wish my Mum could relax a little but understand why she is like this and I don't resent her for it – Tom's needs are the number one priority in her life and for this I admire her.

* See 'Terms you may come across' on page 39.

> "It's hard going out with friends because she wants a constant commentary on where I am, what I'm doing and who I'm with!"
>
> Carys

27

QUESTIONS PEOPLE OFTEN ASK...

Is autism an illness?
Autism is not an illness and cannot be 'caught' by contact with someone who has it. You cannot die of it, either. Autism is a developmental condition. People with autism are usually born with it and it can be recognised by the presence of difficulty in three areas: communication (not just talking – non verbal communication too), social skills (interacting with other people – and knowing what someone else is feeling) and flexible thinking (imagining what may happen next, or how people may react in certain circumstances, as well as adapting to new information and coping with change).

Can people be cured of autism?
As far as we know, if someone has autism they will always have it, because it is caused by the way their brain works. This affects their way of thinking and makes them who they are. It is not always a negative thing, however, and many people with it are rightly proud of their skills, eg good memory, sense of humour, honesty and lack of malice.

Is Asperger syndrome a type of autism?
Yes, it is. Asperger syndrome was named after Hans Asperger, an Austrian doctor who studied a group of children with unusual behaviour as part of his research in 1944. All the children in his group had average or above average intelligence, (he called them his 'little professors' because of their detailed knowledge of favourite subjects!) So the name is generally used for the most able individuals with autism who can speak well.

Do people grow out of their autism or will they always have autism?
Autism is a spectrum condition which can affect people to a greater or lesser degree. People who have autism can also have other disabilities, too. Many of the difficulties it creates can be overcome with the right support. Whilst some individuals who are severely affected by their autism (and possibly other disabilities) remain dependent on others all their lives, others at the other end of the spectrum can go on to lead successful independent lives. People with autism can live happy, fulfilled lives.

What help is there for people with autism when they grow up?
Adults with autism are entitled to seek help and support from social services to ensure that their needs are met, for example, help with housing, money to pay for essential care and services to access. There are also many autism-specific voluntary organisations who work together with social services to offer sheltered or supported housing and employment. Adults with autism go on learning and improving well into their adult lives.

What causes autism?
It is not known for certain what causes autism and this question is the subject of research throughout the world. Some people think it is an inherited condition, others that it can be induced by harmful substances in the bloodstream before or after birth. It may be that some people are more prone to develop autism than others, but there may be particular triggers. It may well be that there is more than one cause.

Many newspapers have given a high profile to the role of the MMR (measles and rubella) vaccination as a possible cause of autism. However, there has been disagreement between scientists on whether this is true. Recent research has concluded that the vaccine does not cause autism, although a number of parents have reported a marked change in their child's behaviour after vaccination. However, the age when autistic behaviour first becomes noticeable happens to coincide with the age when babies commonly receive their first immunisation, so it has not been an easy task to make a clear judgement.

How many people have autism?

Current figures suggest that roughly one in 100 of the UK population have a diagnosis of an autism spectrum disorder, around 500,000 people in total. This may not be an entirely accurate picture, however, because of the problems of gathering accurate information. What is becoming clear is that most UK primary schools have several children on the autism spectrum.

There are certainly more people with a diagnosis of autism than there used to be, as in the 1960s and 1970s it was considered rare. The increase in numbers is partly because it is easier to get a diagnosis and because more people recognise the signs of the condition. However, studies show that there has been no increase in the number of people diagnosed with what is sometimes called classic or Kanner autism. Now more people are diagnosed who are not also profoundly affected by a number of learning difficulties – those diagnosed with, for example, high functioning autism (HFA) or Asperger syndrome.

What is the connection between autism and dyspraxia?

Dyspraxia is a condition in which a person has difficulty with some movements and gestures, especially those requiring two hands or feet such as riding a bike. It can vary in degree but will usually be seen as clumsiness or lack of dexterity rather than a serious physical problem. It is fairly common for people on the autism spectrum to have dyspraxia because the same area of the brain is involved in both. In fact, many people on the autism spectrum often have other neurological developmental difficulties, eg dyslexia, dyscalculia and dyspraxia.

Are there any famous people who have or had autism?

There are a lot of famous people from the past who are now suspected to have been on the autism spectrum but who didn't have a diagnosis because the condition hadn't been given a name during their lifetime, eg the composer Mozart, the scientist Albert Einstein and professor of mathematics and author of Alice in Wonderland, Lewis Carroll. Present day famous people with a diagnosis include British singer/song writer Gary Numan, American Pulitzer prize winning critic and author Tim Page, Nobel Laureate in Economics Vernon L. Smith, British architectural artist Stephen Wiltshire and solo singer Ladyhawke.

Is there a genetic test for autism?

It is thought that there is a genetic element associated with autism, but it is not caused by a single gene. Scientists think a combination of several different genes may be involved. In 2009, some progress was made in isolating a number of genes that may play a part in autism. There is no genetic test for autism yet and developing one is likely to prove difficult. This is because of the varying number and combination of genes that may cause the condition. Environmental factors may also influence whether people with those genes develop autism. Although there are families where more than one member has autism, this is not always the case.

Is there a name for people who don't have autism?

Some people with autism refer to people who haven't as 'neurotypicals', ie people with a typical brain or way of thinking. They often find them difficult to understand! ■

You may recognise some of the situations in the real life stories included here and on pages 6, 7, 22, 27 and 38.

What's the matter with your brother?

Victoria is two years older than her brother who has Asperger syndrome and is now in his early 20s.

"What's the matter with your brother?" If only I had a penny for every time I was asked that. It's an important thing being part of 'the crowd' as a teenager. The problem was that the crowd saw how different he was.

The crowd had noticed my brother wore the same clothes every day, ate nothing but Coco Pops, wouldn't sleep alone, was selfish, unsociable, and obsessed with egg timers.

Everyday activities were planned by my mum and me with military precision, for example, shopping - otherwise there'd be screaming and trashing of Sainsbury's. We would leave stressed and red-faced, with old ladies telling us: "He needs a good smacking, dear."

Changes in routine or life that seemed small to us would smash his world into little pieces of chaos which we patiently put back together again. My mum involved me with everything we did to help him, which provided me with a sense of understanding so I never felt pushed out as

> "If someone gave me a magic wand and said I could have an average brother, I'd give it back."
>
> Victoria

30

some siblings do. I've no idea what it's like to have an 'average' brother because it's just him and me, but if someone gave me a magic wand and said I could have an average brother, I'd give it back. He is who he is and I'm proud of him. He's taught me so much: tolerance, patience, understanding, persistence, strength, I can explain one thing a million different ways, I don't do panic, I think on my feet and outside the box, and I've learned to laugh. If he wasn't who he was I wouldn't be who I am. He's better than an average brother any day!

Victoria now works for The National Autistic Society in its residential services and says, "My brother is the single reason I wanted my job."

FIND THESE...
DYSLEXIA • AUTISM • KANNER • GLUTEN FREE DIET
ASPERGER SYNDROME • COMMUNICATION • EMPATHY
MEASLES • ALLERGY • MEMORY • DYSPRAXIA
HYPERLEXIA • HIGH FUNCTIONING • SEROTONIN
SOCIAL STORIES • SENSITIVITY • HYPERACTIVITY
ATTENTION DEFICIT

BULLYING

All of us experience bullying at some time – deliberate, repeated behaviour which makes us uncomfortable, sad, hurt or afraid. Your brother or sister may be bullied for being different, and it's possible that you could be bullied for having a brother or sister who is different. It's important to be able to deal with this.

People with autism are often the victims of bullying, maybe because they look like everyone else, so others don't make allowances for their difficulties. They get singled out for behaving differently even though they can't help it. Bullying can range from mild to potentially life-threatening, but it is never acceptable.

Anthony

Damian

Lisa

Bullying behaviour	Example	Effect on victim
Exclude person from group	Talk openly in front of someone about a party to which they are not invited.	Feel isolated, unpopular "What's wrong with me?"
Laugh at someone's confusion/clumsiness/ignorance	Jeer at someone because they wear their shirt tucked in, or when they trip.	Hurt, feel unattractive and awkward.
Take advantage of someone's poor understanding	Encourage someone to break a school rule, then run away and let them get caught.	Feel confused, humiliated, betrayed, stupid. "I thought he liked me."
Name calling	Call someone a "*******!!!"	Feel hurt, humiliated. Sense of injustice: "That's not true!"
Insult person's close family	"Your mother's a *******!!"	Sense of outrage, anger.
Break a promise	Fail to turn up when you have arranged to meet and they don't apologise about it.	Distress: "Where are they? They must hate me." Anger. Self-pity.
Damage property	Write swear words all over someone's bag in felt tip.	Worry. "I can't use that now. What will mum say?" Anger. Distress.
Theft	Take someone's school book.	Fear of getting into trouble. Helplessness. Feel wretched and hated.
Physical abuse	Kick or punch someone out of sight of adults then run off.	Physical pain. Fear. Feeling of helplessness, humiliation: "I must be awful for them to do this to me."
Cyber bullying	Poisonous or obscene texts or emails.	Fear. Unable to escape. Feel hated, unclean.

1. **IT'S NEVER OK TO BE BULLIED. Don't accept it as normal.**

2. Tell an adult (a teacher if you are at school). Be prepared to name/describe the bully.

3. Don't retaliate with the same behaviour or it will escalate.

4. Think of strategies for avoiding being in a vulnerable position, eg take a different route home, stay near sympathetic people or find a safe place at break times (use the school buddy system if there is one).

5. Think about skills which could be learnt to increase confidence and reduce the likelihood of being targeted, eg martial arts, telling jokes, sports which build strength and fitness. Take a look at the information sheet produced by the NAS for young people with autism as it may be helpful – see www.autism.org.uk/bullies

6. Remember: victims are not bad. It's the bullying that's bad.

NO-ONE HAS ANY TIME FOR ME in our house. My younger sister, aged four, still behaves like a toddler and my older brother with his autism is like a baby even though he's 17. I feel as if my parents don't care about me. What shall I do to make them notice me?

Don't make the mistake of thinking you have to behave extra well to get noticed – or really badly either for that matter! It's really important that you talk to your parents about how you feel. Don't feel guilty about getting on with your own life and spending time with your friends away from your family, but try to put aside a bit of time each day for your family too. Maybe sitting to watch TV with your brother – he's bound to like something that you also find amusing, eg cartoons. Take a look at the section 'Coping with parents' on p26 for some more tips, too.

MY BROTHER'S BEHAVIOUR is so embarrassing that I can't bring my friends home. How can I explain to them why he keeps taking his clothes off (even though he's 14) and wears only boxer shorts in the house even in mid winter?

You need to explain to your friends that one of the characteristics of autism is that it makes people react differently to sensory information. Your brother may find it difficult to tolerate the sensation of feeling hot or the scratchiness of some clothing. You can also explain that because of his autism he isn't aware of how he appears to others.

I'M SO FED UP. Our family life is limited by what my sister can't cope with, eg because of her fear of planes, we can never go abroad. Surely she needs to be made to face up to her fears or she'll never get over them?

Your sister's fear is very overwhelming – if you have a fear of spiders or snakes you probably know what it might feel like – but unlike you, she is unlikely to be easily comforted by other people. It may be that she can be helped to manage her fears with the help of someone (not emotionally involved with her) like a psychologist or counsellor with experience of autism. However, this is likely to take time. Have you talked to your mum and dad about your feelings? You could try mentioning to them that the Autism Helpline (0845 070 4004) may be able to help, and that it has information about holidays and preparing to go away. You could also say that some airports have special centres which can help introduce people to airport procedures and flying. Have you thought, too, about whether there are any other opportunities for you to go away, for example, with friends?

WE CAN NEVER BE SPONTANEOUS in our house! Everything has to be planned with military precision or my brother has a massive tantrum. Is there some way that we can teach him to enjoy doing things on the spur of the moment – like not watching TV and going out to a show with friends who unexpectedly have a spare ticket? Unfortunately, enjoying new experiences depends on having an understanding of the world which people on the autism spectrum take longer to get. Until they have that understanding they need to be taught that it is OK to change the routine occasionally. Something as simple as drawing two pictures: one of you all sitting happily watching a show and another of you watching a recorded version of the TV show later can be enough to make them relaxed enough to try the new thing. This would give them time to work it out – time which they don't have if you simply say you're doing it.

I DON'T KNOW WHAT I CAN DO with my brother – he's only interested in fantasy books/games and seems to watch and play the same things over and over. I wish I had a sister I could share secrets with – it feels lonely at home sometimes. Does he know I have thoughts and feelings and will he ever see me as a person and be able to understand me?
People on the autism spectrum have difficulty understanding and expressing their own feelings and for this reason find it more relaxing to spend time on repetitive activities (like watching favourite DVDs) rather than talking to other people. You may be able to help him by trying to explain to him how you feel in different ways, eg after he has upset you, rate your anger on a scale of 1 to 10; draw a picture of yourself with big tears; or write him a note saying 'I am cross because...' He may learn to communicate back to you in the same way in time. Remember that he will go on improving and learning well into adult life, so don't give up on him. It's a marathon not a sprint!

Since my brother was diagnosed with Asperger syndrome two years ago, my parents seem to use it as an excuse for his behaviour. The other day he hit me just because I said I couldn't give him his usual Saturday evening game of chess as I made plans to go out with friends, but they didn't even tell him off. If he's clever enough to play chess surely he's clever enough to understand that people can't always do what he wants?
Understanding people is a very different skill from playing chess. Although your brother appears a typical teenager on the outside, on the inside he thinks in a very different way from you – and always will. When plans change he cannot adapt quickly, nor can he imagine why your friends are more important to you than your regular chess game. Try to explain to him how you feel and he may understand you better next time. It's important to say to your parents that you feel that he needs to know that hitting people is wrong and that it hurts. If you need to change plans for the chess game in future and know about this some time beforehand, then it may a good idea to prepare him in advance and offer an alternative time for the game.

I SOMETIMES LOOK AT MY MUM and wonder how she manages to cope with my sister (17, with classic autism) on her own. She looks shattered most of the time because she never gets a full night's sleep. I dread what will happen when she is no longer around and fear I will be expected to look after my sister. I don't want to be tied down and wish I could feel free to plan my own future as an air steward. Am I just selfish or do others feel the same as me?
The fact that you have asked the question shows that you care about your sister and have a sense of duty. Of course you should follow your dreams and ambitions. Your sister is not your sole responsibility. The state is there to provide the basics and there are voluntary organisations which can help to provide the extra things to enhance her quality of life. Maybe your role could be to help speak up for what she wants if she can't do so for herself. Why not widen the circle of people who know her by having a party for her and see if they can come up with some ideas about including her in new activities, eg swimming or walking? ■

BOOKS
Some of the books below are aimed at siblings of people with autism, some are for young people with autism – and could be useful to you too, and some are of general interest. You can find some of the following titles on the NAS website: www.autism.org.uk/shop

Different like me: my book of autism heroes Jennifer Elder. Jessica Kingsley Publishers, 2006

Everybody is different: a book for young people who have brothers and sisters with autism Fiona Bleach. The National Autistic Society, 2001

Freaks, geeks and Asperger syndrome Luke Jackson. Jessica Kingsley Publishers, 2002

I really don't know why: a sibling song to autism Haitham-Al-Ghani. The National Autistic Society, 2007

My family is different: a workbook for children with a brother or sister who has autism or Asperger syndrome Carolyn Brock. The National Autistic Society, 2007

Truth or dare Celia Rees. Macmillan Children's Books, 2000

What did you say? What do you mean? An illustrated guide to understanding metaphors Jude Welton. Jessica Kingsley Publishers, 2002

DVDs
Autism and me Rory Hoy. Jessica Kingsley Publishers, 2007

Asperger syndrome: a different mind Simon Baron-Cohen. Jessica Kingsley Publishers, 2007

INTERNET
Information for siblings of all ages is available on the NAS website at: www.autism.org.uk/siblingsinfo
It includes links to a range of interesting sites, including some web forums/chat rooms for siblings.

REAL LIFE STORY

> "Some days I wonder who I would be if it wasn't for the autism..."
> **Amy**

You may recognise some of the situations in the real life stories included here and on pages 6, 7, 22, 27 and 30.

Living with my sister

Amy writes about her sister Sophie.

In order to make sense of her world, Sophie likes order. Her bedroom is her sanctuary. She can line her things up in the precise way she wants. She gets anxious if her routine is disrupted. Like me, she's quite a worrier. Living with someone with autism makes you realise how everybody has a slight autistic tendency. People are just very good at covering it up.

If everyone understood human emotions like Sophie, the world would be far less complicated. She'll tell you when she's upset with you. She couldn't begin to understand why you would want to hide something like that. She gives inanimate objects personalities, like her iPod speakers. They get a headache if the volume is too loud. It makes sense to me.

Sophie left her 16+ unit this summer and is due to start an independence learning-for-work course at our local college. Maybe next year I'll be joining her to do my art foundation year. It will be nice to be together. We can make lunch dates in the canteen.

I'm nervous about the future, and about Sophie's sheer vulnerability within the world. Although my friends have always been very accepting of Sophie, I still find it incredibly difficult to talk about her. I just don't know where to begin.

I think, subconsciously, I have grown within myself as a result of my sister. Some days I wonder who I would be if it wasn't for the autism. Other days I don't want to know. I know I wouldn't be me without Sophie in my life. ■